The Red Book
Musings of a Manic Depressive
Phase: Manic

Works by Aaron Rogier

Aleph-Sub-Aleph Press
http://www.aaronrogier.net/alephsubaleph

This work is a collection of poetry from
a manic phase of the author. For some readers
the material contained within may be a bit intense
or trigger strong emotional response.

I publish this work in defiance of the stigma
that is thrust upon so many persons.

The Red Book

All Rights Reserved
Copyright 2009 Anno Domini
Aaron Rogier

ISBN: 978-0-578-01314-5
Library of Congress Control Number: 2009901776

For Information about the Author visit
http://www.aaronrogier.net

Aleph-Sub-Aleph is a
Publishing imprint of the author
For more information visit
http://www.aaronrogier.net/alephsubaleph

Table of Contents

Foreword	1
Bright Light	3
Motion	4
Abode	5
Map of the United States	6
Stairs	7
Homeostasis	8
Caves	9
Kindling	10
Kindle Harder	11
Calm	12
Break the Dam	13
Respite	14
Want	15
Pact	16
Cold	17
Twinkle	18
Haze	19
Pangloss	20
Flight	21
Pretense, Illusion	22
Down	23
Abide	24
Pools	25
Still	26

Hymn #1 (Glue)	27
Smolder	28
Resignation	29
Αθανατοσ (Undying)	30
Drizzle	31
Trapped Flames	32
Treachery	33
Long	34
Hymn #2 (Glory)	35
Requiem for Zyprexa	36
Hymn #3 (Aaron Man)	37
Locke's Rock	38
Revolution	39
Let Go	40
Torn	41
Fast	42
Postscript	43
Appendix	44

Foreword

There is great stigma attached to the subject I am taking on in this book. I acknowledge that and thrust this work into the world in spite of ill considered value judgments that may be made by others who would judge my integrity, character, or ability for the theme addressed within this book. Still further I deplore those who would make a negative judgment about my worth as a human being for the subject addressed and my openness in working towards addressing it.

I have suffered great depression. This collection of poetry is about my experience with an experience with an adversary darker and more deceptive than the depression. It is about my experience with a mania or hypomania. Pinning down exactly what it is and how far it wanted to go would be impossible as I went to seek treatment fairly early in its course.

Untreated mental illness leads to pain, not only for the afflicted, but additionally to all of those around them who get caught in the spiral of suffering. I am fortunate to have a supportive family. I am fortunate to have a good education. I am especially fortunate that a medical intervention was possible early on in the course of the mania.

I must admit that my hopes were not high for the amount and quality of support that would be available. For my great depressions the support available often seemed distant and disinterested. As a result there was great pain for myself and others.

This collection of poetry I submit to the world in the Heraclitian tradition. It is one matter to read about something. It leads to knowing *about* something.

It is another matter entirely to immerse yourself into an experience as a matter of trying to truly *know* something. I am a firm believer in the difference between knowledge about and knowledge of. The difference may seem subtle, but it is an entire world apart to experience the difference.

The references to the fire are a tribute to the great philosopher Heraclitus. They are also a very apt way to describe the force with which the brain pushes and does consume the mind within the manic state.

I also do personify some of the medications in the poetry, as they are indeed critical characters to the story of the subduction of the mania. Despite their efforts and successes in keeping one level, they do not entirely eliminate the struggle with one's own treasonous brain. It is a scary occasion when the organ of thought and knowing turns against you.

To those who suffer the brains treason, and the stigma I dedicate this work. To those who have offered their help and support I additionally dedicate this work. To those who have suffered with a treasonous brain or suffered with those who have a treasonous brain, I do dedicate this work.

Aaron J. Rogier

Bright Light

Bright under night
Glows the maniac's bedroom Light
Bright the maniac himself must burn
Lest he suffer Gloom's return

    Hotter, Hotter, his mind does kindle
    For even with Lilly's swindle
    Little calm is wrought
    From the dot the maniac sought

Burning hotter, the fire kindles
Deep, fast, the monoamines boil
Oceans roil in Galactic coil
In the dark of night
Deprived of light
The Maniac packs his daily bindle

Motion

Flying about in Brownian dance
A Grey world thrown Askance
Grey ashes of a fire burnt
Embers glow of lessons learnt
Even ash from volcanic terror
Becomes all mud with rain
Of Sorrows leaden pain
All is mud the same

Abode

In his small off white box
While others sleep he is awake
Safe behind a deadbolt lock
The maniac retreats to a world of thoughts
A world which quakes
In search of placid lakes

Map of the United States

Colored Blotches
Watery Crotches
A Spider's web of Roads
Oh what a map holds

Stairs

Winding up cave like stairs
Begrudging all hopes and cares
Returning Beelzebub's stare

The ascent past Satan's Lair
Through the cold gray void
Avoiding the noid

Venture towards χαοσ

Homeostasis

Fire lights every Sun
All the while lighting every Son
Fresh like a baker's finest bun
Freely the Sun's fire on the run
So to the fire of the Son

Both are driven to deep water
With the fire water does boil

    Fearing the intent of the matter

The boil does roil
As everything mud then does dry
With steam's hissing cry
Dusty earth where once mud

    On come clouds and rain

Everything returns to mud.

Caves

      Delving deeper
Pressing further
      Into the watery cave
The hero abides
          With the sight of his light
      Pressing further
          To a watery grave
   Our hero
          Stutters
                  Stops
   Turns to face
      Several mud pots
Warm breeze from the pots
      Sets his lantern wick to   Stop

No Light
      By the heat of the pots
      Our hero
         Finds
   His own personal hell

         At least its warmer than the damp, dark

   Cave

Kindling

Kindle, Kindle the fire still Kindles
Tinder long gone the fire still Kindles

    From Embers Lost
        To Embers Found

Kindling down
To hard ground

    The fire burns
    All consumed
    Fearing the return
    Of dark gloom

    The fire kindles
        Burning bright

Kindle Harder

Kindle, Kindle, the fire still kindles
The tinder long gone the Kindle continues
Stown away the fuel into a bindle
Burning the bindle the Kindle continues

    The kindle continues its new fuel a rage
    All is caught in horrendous churn
    Alas how bright the fire burns
    My the kindle please find a cage

May control find this twisted rage
Still hope ensues
That for fire a cage
Still though fear of the blue

Calm

Lo, here comes Zyprexa's calm
Swift Zyprexa's wrath
Brings forth a slow smooth path
Hope so small fits on a palm

    Lo here a peaceful psalm
    Winding on untrodden path
    Engaging in newfound math
    Lilly's hammer brings forth calm.

        Lo by Zyprexa's wrath
        A calming spell was cast

Break the Dam

Fire burns
Cosumes the dam
Pile still more bags of sand

Watch the dam crumble to sand
A light is the dam
Fire Burnt

Respite

Play with words
Creates a world
A wind to escape
To other worlds
Trying to leave
The Fire's burn

      This is but
      A brief respite
      Though the fire
      Still burns bright

            Wow the fire
            How it burns
            And throw worlds
I   On the Pyre

Want

How the fire twists one's needs
From ego to id raising the deepest greed
From dark to light a seed
Sprouting unrequited need
Sprouting profound need

From what was once
Just merely want

Pact

A pact is made
Ativan comes to Zyprexa's aid
Even with the force they made
The fire still did not abate

      Through all this aid
      By Pharma made

   My brain feels as though a drain

Cold

Even in cold dark of night
Still the fire does burn bright
Many things in this night
Readily catch alight

    Even in the coldest night
    Too much is still alight

Twinkle

Twinkle, Twinkle, little star
I once wondered what you are
How your gasses
Burn so nuclear, bright
Though eventually you too stop
Causing great Galactic blight

Haze

From the haze
Returns manic twisted blaze
For all life must be saved

From the dying of the night
Return's the Sun's empowering light
Lifting fog with its great light
For the dying of the night

The sun shadows over bleak twilight
For soon will birth yet another night
With the passing dying of the light

The dying of the Sun's great light
Leaves Son lost in haze

Pangloss

In torment caught
What is, not ought
What should not, be

Among the largest trees
With axes some are hewn
Some far too soon

Behold Gödel's riddle
Is the world consistent
Or complete in its existence

Flight

What bird does fly
But does not land

From the Sky
Down to the Sand

At least the bird
Chooses when to land

But what of the fish
Which must swim
Until its end

Pretense, Illusion

The actors cry
All the world's a stage
No I say, In fisted rage

There are no scenes
There are no acts
Props and sets cannot be found
There is no mixer for the sound

N o plot, No performance
There is no practice

There only is

Down

For now I fly
But must soon land

Maybe soft earth
Maybe soft sand

Hard shale rock?

Please no Ocean

Deep, blue, cold, vest, wet

Abide

Flat, tranquil, calm
Respite before the storm

Klonopin at my side
This dude will abide

Lo this vicious storm
It has so many eyes

How I despise the form
Though I welcome the eyes

And so I will abide
With Klonopin at my side
Zyprexa holding strong
I pray the eye will hold long

Pools

From cold deep pools
The storm has come to rule

While Satan's crowned with jewels
My thorny crown turns inside
I approach the storm in stride
Facing dark cold pools

Still

Behind the storm
Past fiery Tempest winds
The pools still lies
Deep, Dark, Cold
Waiting to pull me in
Once more, again

A tempest all its own
Is the stillness of the pool
There is no fear
This place I already know
This still tempest of gloom

Hymn (Glue)

The laurel wreath

Placed upon his storied brow

Tossed aside

After the race

Who knew of reward

For last place

The laurel wreath

Is ready now

To lift up from

His troubled brow

Smolder

Tranquil smoke
Where's the mote
Still alight
Feel the heat
Something is still alight
Despite Zyprexa's might
Fire still burns
The world still churns
For peace, I still yearn

Resignation

For all of Zyprexa's might
Still no dying of things alight
Though the flames have cooled
Though yet no fall to depression's pool

There is no rage, no rage,
    Against the dying of things alight
        For still embers burn

Could still kindle again the fire
Consuming the world with greater ire
There is no rage for the dying of things alight

Αθανατοσ (Undying)

Rage, Rage, Rage
Hot the fire burns
As passes the day
As the flames rise high
Αθανατοσ! The fire lives
No rivers quench
This fire's thirst
Αθανατοσ its φυςισ
From itself the fire burns
For all the fire burns
From ash comes all

Drizzle

Day is Flame

Night is Ash

In turn each does pass

From ground to cloud

Water does travel

From cloud to ground

Water rains

Still, in spite of Flame's reign

Trapped Flames

Oh how the fire is slight

    Striving Higher
    The flames burn

        Trapped within
        Zyprexa's Block

Klonopin can quell its steam
The fire still does dream

    So I am weary
    Yet still dry

        Still Outside
            Depression's pool

Treachery

In treachery
Men turn against each other

    What then?

        When the mind
          turns against oneself

Control does slip
Impulses grip

Ghastly business
Wrestling one's own brain

Long

Long have I known
The brains treason
Which leaves me down

    Still now a greater treason
    When the brain abdicates
    Its bony throne

Terrifying is the sight, the feel
Uncontrolled Euphoria

So I take my pills
To feel just alright

    Still the traitor
    Revises its plot

Hymn #2 (Glory)

Mine eyes have seen the glory
Of rampant euphoria
It has loosened up my smile
Which my other affects abhorred

Kindling, burning
The mania still goes on

Kindling, burning
The mania still goes on

From the darkest pits
of depression and despair
The fire which has kindled
breaks down barriers

Social, Ethical, Financial
Even Pharmaceutical

The mania marches on

Requiem for Zyprexa

Where Zyprexa failed
Now Risperdal is availed

While the coals still glow
Far less the flames do grow

From a book relief was sought
An adequate right dose

Though the hold's not perfect
I must tolerate defect

I still feel the trap
In which I'm caught
Surrounded in a smolder of crap

Hymn #3 (Aaron Man)

For I am Aaron Man
Filled with little more than dread

My heavy brain is full of lead

I am Aaron Man
Broken is the seal
For my torment is revealed

I am Aaron Man
Poisoned is my broken Mind

Locke's Rock

John Lock's
Blank slate rock
Can just muck
In the river's crevasse
Just like Buridan's Ass

For the brain has organic structure
From which the mind may not escape
Even with the longest reach
Of its greatest cognitive seek

Revolution

Revolution in my mind
Am I finding peace
Am I blind
In a field of geese

I know no longer what I fear
Sweet music I do hear

Travel far enough east
In the west you'll feast

How my mind
Is not blind
And without fail
Ought soon return

Let Go

Let go my ego
To let it go

    Free

        Let it free
        Just let it be

So much to do
I will see it through

Living just for living
Being simply Being

Torn

Feeling torn inside
I must keep up my stride

To lift my life
Above the strife

My tortured mind
How I know its kind

I think I have it
In a bind

So I take it slow
And enjoy the flow

Fast

Heart is racing
Mind is speeding

Pen is flowing
Anxiety growing

Out here I feel so cold
So young and yet so old
Could it be the fire's out
Somehow I still have doubt

Postscript

Well as I write this concluding statement I am still in the midst of my struggle to conquer my manic depressive illness. It is like anything else in life. Very rarely is one ever eased into anything. We are thrust into the world in the midst of the muck and each of us is to carve out a hollow in the muck of the world on their own.

Sometimes I wonder at what point in history it became something other than mere survival which was taken up to be the new sense of thriving. I wonder when it became not simply enough to continue to persevere in being, but to do so at a degree so far removed from that which is simply necessary to sustain life.

That is beyond this scope though, and could be a work all its own.

Appendix

For information about mental health on the web, the following are some sites that provide helpful resources.

Crazy Meds

http://www.crazymeds.us

This is the best resource for information on psychiatric medications and their applications to treat problems online.

The San Francisco Review of Mental Health

http://www.themedmagazine.com

A humorous and satirical online magazine by the mentally interesting for the mentally interesting, The San Francisco Review of Mental Health is an excellent respite from so much of the disempowering literature out there

Then there are the various support groups etcetera which are too numerous to mention.

www.ingramcontent.com/pod-product-compliance
Lightning Source LLC
Chambersburg PA
CBHW022343040426
42449CB00006B/691